BOOK OF BASEBALL STUFF

Other Books in This Series

BOOK OF FOOTBALL STUFF

BOOK OF
Baseball
Stuff

Ron Martirano

Illustrated by Mike McCoy

imagine!
New York
www.imaginebks.com

Text and art copyright © 2009 by Imagine Publishing, Inc.

Published by Imagine Publishing, Inc.
25 Whitman Road, Morganville, NJ 07751

Distributed in the United States of America by
BookMasters Distribution Services, Inc.
30 Amberwood Parkway, Ashland, OH 44805

Distributed in Canada by
BookMasters Distribution Services, Inc.
c/o Jacqueline Gross Associates, 165 Dufferin Street,
Toronto, Ontario, Canada M6K 3H6

Distributed in the United Kingdom by
Publishers Group UK
8 The Arena, Mollison Avenue, Enfield, EN3 7NL, UK

ISBN-10: 0-9822939-9-2
ISBN-13: 978-0-9822939-9-7

Library of Congress Control Number: 2009922013

Designed by Marc Cheshire
Printed in China
1 3 5 7 9 10 8 6 4 2

To my one and only love,
my wonderful wife, Erica

Contents

Introduction

What makes baseball work as a pastime is that no matter the standings or the outcome, every game has the potential to connect with the past. Whether it's the ballpark tradition or the unexpected play that hasn't been seen in years, for each fan there exists a thread connecting every element of their baseball life. Some see it through the history of their favorite team or player, but it's rarely a single side of the game that makes up anyone's experience. What brings it all together is the assemblage of random elements and events that each of us collects as we watch season after season. These go beyond the pedestrian facts gleamed off a ballpark scoreboard; they are the stored memories that sometimes only nine innings of ball can resuscitate. While none of us has the same collection, if you bring together a roomful of real fans and get them talking, the excitement over a shared understanding would make like a secret handshake for an exclusive club. It's not the recital of stats or the memorization of lineup cards that grants access, but the sampling of baseball stuff across a wide spectrum.

What you hold in your hands is just that: baseball stuff from every corner of the game. Inside you'll find an assortment of stories and forgotten moments—all of the sort that might be told after some excited fan exclaims, "Remember the time? . . ." Completing that memory are details that most of us forgot we even knew until we were prompted. The game prompts us every night, allowing each of us to dig back to unimaginable depths at unexpected moments. This collection aspires to tap into the shared recesses and retrieve the plays and players we all get excited about.

Perhaps more than anything else, being reminded of that which others might consider obscure, produces a strong reaction in each of us—because it ultimately brings us back home. After all, who but a diehard fan would celebrate the games that go beyond the championships won? Any bandwagon fan can tune into Game 7 of a postseason series, but it's the ins and outs of the 162-game season that get us there. Going back is going home, and its not only fun, but, when all is said and done, it's the object of the game.

Unusual
Stuff

OUTSIDE of the experiences of frequent-flying, season-ticket holders, most fans are guided through their baseball journey by play-by-play men, color commentators, radio talk-show hosts, sportswriters, and blog moderators. These field-level experts (some more knowledgeable than others) relay and interpret the action while providing a historical context. Harry Carey led Chicago baseball fans on both sides of that city's league divide. Dodger fans in both Brooklyn and Los Angeles have had the time between pitches filled by the great Vin Scully. In Boston, Jerry Remy. Bob Murphy, Tim McCarver, Phil Rizzutto, Keith Hernandez, and John Sterling have all provided the soundtrack for the epic battles engaged by New York's fabled teams. We invite these voices into our homes, we read their perspectives on events we have just seen, and we sing along with their battle cries with

Oh, it's a long one! It's going . . . going . . . it's really gone!

each long fly ball that is high, that is far, that is . . . sometimes caught.

Whichever transmission you find yourself on the receiving end of, whichever subscription you devour daily, baseball is a 162-part serial (sometimes 181), repeated year in and year out, and its narrators love to shine a spotlight on those rare or previously unseen moments. What follows are not bookmarks in the record book, but rather footnotes and asterisks. These are the wide world of sports moments, some that live on in rain-delay highlight reels, others tucked away until the next bad hop or errant throw revives them into relevancy.

Nine innings to play (occasionally less and sometimes more), twenty-seven outs per side (twenty-four at the plate on a good night for the home team), three-game series after three-game series (the schedule-teasing two and rarely satisfying four not withstanding)—and just as it seems that monotony might be on deck, a bird gets in the way. As Mel Allen used to say, "How about that!?"

CLASSICALLY ODD

Part of what gives baseball its charm are the characters it draws. The golden age of the game may have been profitable for owners, but the game was not yet big business. More relaxed times allowed for a different standard, and made for some good stories as well.

No Arguments Here

Some umpires have been accused of a hair-trigger temper when it comes to dealing with those who disagree with their calls. Thankfully, this proved to be furthest from the truth during a potentially deadly dispute during a nineteenth-century game between two local New Jersey teams, Clifton and Little Falls. As the story has been

18

Go ahead. Make my day.

told, one of the pitchers, named Connelly, was feeling squeezed by the umpire, Mahoney. Connelly eventually got so frustrated that, with a bat in hand, he confronted the ump. In response, Mahoney reportedly produced a revolver he had hidden in his inside coat pocket, and shoved it into the hurler's face—suggesting a bad ending would follow if Connelly proceeded. Connelly saw the wisdom of Mahoney's position and returned to the mound.

Over the Wall

While Manny Ramirez was once late returning to his position after slipping away inside Boston's Green Monster for a quick bathroom break, he wasn't the first outfielder to find relief behind the outfield wall. Over a century before Manny was Manny, St. Louis Brown outfielder Curt Welch apparently enjoyed nothing more than a cold bottle of suds on hot day. (So much so that he once reportedly dedicated a season to his beverage of choice.) As other players have no doubt learned since, it's difficult to get a concession worker into the outfield.

Oops. I better get that.

So, Welch saw a problem and found a solution. The three-time American Association league leader in times hit by pitch hid cases of beer behind the Sportsman's Park billboards. Considering his propensity for getting hit by pitches, perhaps he should have shared.

Theft Deterrence

German Schaefer was the sort of clownish character that baseball seems to eternally draw—so much so that this turn-of-the-century player found an off-season career on the vaudeville stage. Among his on-the-field antics, he's perhaps best known for the unusual feat of having successfully stolen first base. Around 1911, during the ninth inning of a tie game against the White Sox, Schaefer, playing for the Senators, stood on first with the go-ahead run on third. Schaefer took second base unchallenged. But with two outs, a speedy run-

Get him! He's a diamond thief!

ner on third, and a lack of confidence in the batter at
the plate, he made a unique bid to cash in on the rally.
On the next pitch, Schaefer broke back for first base, to
the confusion of the Chicago infield and the delight of

the crowd. The play was as comical as it was strategic, since it was designed to draw a throw from the catcher and give the runner at third a chance to steal home. No throw came, and the inning ended with the game still tied. Washington, however, did manage to pull it out in the twelfth, and the rules were subsequently changed to deter similar antics.

"I Don't Know" Is on Third . . .
and He's Got Company

While the Brooklyn Dodgers are best remembered as being affectionately referred to as "Dem Bums" by their most loyal, the team was also referred to as the "Daffiness Boys." The play most emblematic of their reputation occurred in 1926 in a game against the Braves (then in Boston). It began with a single in the bottom of the seventh from Dodger infielder Johnny Butler. Butler scored on a double from Brooklyn backstop Hank DeBerry. With DeBerry on second, pitcher Dazzy Vance singled, advancing him to third. The bases were then loaded when Chick Fewster was hit by a pitch. Following Merwin Jacobson's pop out, Babe Herman stepped to the plate.

Herman cracked a line drive and smelled triple out of the box. DeBerry scored easily. While Fewster took off from first, Vance held up for a moment from second to ensure Herman's ball dropped in, and then ran hard. Rounding third and halfway down the line, Vance thought better of breaking for the plate and turned back. Fewster, seeing Vance turn the corner but failing to notice his retreat, headed in to third, only to be greeted by Vance. At that moment, Herman, who had been running hard all the way, finally looked up while pulling in to third base, only to discover he had

Yet another circus act brought to you by Dem Bums.

company. Not only were Vance and Fewster both on third, but so was Ed Taylor, the Boston third baseman—ready to receive the incoming throw from the outfield. Taylor tagged both Vance and Fewster (as the lead runner, Vance was safe), and then doubled up Herman who was on his way back to second. The blunder gave rise to the oft-repeated anecdote of a Dodger fan being excitedly told by another that Brooklyn was rallying with three men on base, only to respond, "Which base?"

Two for the Price of One

During the 1950s, while with the Fort Worth team in the Texas League, Joe Pignatano had become accustomed to his spot in the batting order. He was the team's only catcher and knew he would be in the lineup every day. In fact, both he and teammate Maury Wills had come to expect that if both were playing, each would be in their regular spots in the order—Pignatano seventh, Wills eighth. One day, in a game against Shreveport, Fort Worth manager Tommy Holmes switched the two, only neither bothered checking. Pignatano walked to the plate in his normal spot and promptly hit a home run. By the time he rounded third, Mel McGaha, the opposing manager, had figured out what happened and was waiting at home plate to argue with the umpires. The home run was overturned, and an out was called for batting out of order. The good news for Pignatano was that the eighth spot was now up, so it was his actual turn to bat. He made the best of it by hitting the first pitch he saw over the fence.

A decade later, at the other end of his career (on the second-to-last day of the season), Pignatano made up for the extra at bat. He closed out the season (and his career) by hitting into a triple play.

DEFYING THE ODDS THE OLD-FASHIONED WAY

While controversy still rages today regarding "performance enhancement," various tricks and substances have been in play for as long as the game has been played. These subterfuges were designed to give an advantage, and for each, baseball needed someone willing to cheat to make it a story worth telling. Some prospered; others got caught.

The Pitch Call Seen 'Round the Stadium

As far as stories go, there's something of a perfect storm in play when two rival teams from the same city meet in a deciding playoff game to determine who will advance to the World Series. The storm is even more perfect when the game is decided in a walk-off moment. When cheating allegations surface years later . . . well,

Aaaaaaaaaaaaaaaaaah!

that storm is beyond categorization. The story neither begins nor ends with Ralph Branca and his fateful pitch to New York Giant Bobby Thomson. To set the stage, you need to look back about eight weeks, when on

August 11, 1951, the Brooklyn Dodgers were 13½ games ahead of the Giants in the National League standings. The Giants then proceeded to go on a tear, winning sixteen in a row to pull within six. They then went on a seven-game winning streak in the final week of the season to catch the Dodgers and force a three-game playoff to determine who would play the Yankees in the World Series. (This was, of course, before the modern playoff system was in place.) Having split the first two games, the season would be decided at the Polo Grounds, the Giants' home field.

Brooklyn took a 4-1 lead into the ninth inning, and after scratching out a run and putting two men in scoring position, Bobby Thomson stepped to the plate. Dodger manager Chuck Dressen called on Ralph Branca to face him. Three pitches later, history was made as Thomson hit "the shot heard 'round the world," a line drive down the left field line, only 300 feet from home plate (but far enough to clear the park's short corners and land somewhere in the second deck). New York won 5-4; a "Miracle at Coogan's Bluff" had taken place, and with it, the comeback was complete. Story over?

Not quite.

A few years later, Branca was playing for Detroit, and a teammate that had been with New York in 1951 clued him in to the elaborate sign-stealing system that the Giants had in place—cluing batters in to what pitch was coming next. It started with Giant coach Herman Franks, who, from the vantage point of the center field clubhouse, would use a telescope to read the signs being flashed by the opposing team's catcher. Franks would then use a buzzer to relay to Sal Yvars, the Giants bull-pen catcher, whether a curveball or fastball was coming. (One buzz indicated the curve; otherwise it was assumed to be a heater.) Yvars, visible to the batter at the plate, would use a baseball to bring the message home, telling teammates, "If I hold onto the ball, it's a fastball. If I toss the ball in the air, it's a breaking ball."

Branca kept quiet on the subject, not wanting to sound like a sore loser. When Joshua Prager broke the story for *The Wall Street Journal* fifty years later, Thomson danced around the question as to whether or not he knew what pitch Branca was throwing.

Scratching Out a Win

Rick Honeycutt will never be remembered as "crafty," a description usually reserved for pitchers who managed to put a little something extra on the ball—dirt, spit, Vaseline, whatever. That's not to say Honeycutt didn't try to find an advantage. While playing with the Mariners in 1980, Honeycutt used a bandage to stick a thumbtack to his forefinger, knowing that scratching baseballs gave them extra movement. Umpire Bill Kunkel was alerted to something fishy by Willie Wilson of the Royals, and approached the pitcher to see what was what. Unfortunately, Honeycutt had done such a good job attaching the tack that he couldn't shake it off. When Kunkel grabbed his hand to see if there was something there, he got pricked! To make matters worse, Honeycutt had absently wiped his brow and scratched his forehead, leaving behind a bright red scratch. While there was no blood, he was clearly caught red handed. According to Honeycutt, "I haven't been in trouble like that since the last time I was sent to the principal's office."

A Man of Letters

Don Sutton was known for scuffing pitches. In fact, he once faced a ten-game suspension for defacing the

Sutton's abrasive attitude rubbed umpires the wrong way.

ball (never served). When he and Gaylord Perry (whose reputation for spitballs and other greased pitches was legendary) were teammates, Sutton joked, "He gave me a tube of Vaseline; I thanked him and gave him a piece of sandpaper." With such a reputation, it was no surprise that umpires and opposing managers always kept a close eye on him. Once, while inspecting his glove for sandpaper or any other abrasives, umps instead found a note from Sutton that said, "You're getting warm, but it's not here."

Thinking Outside the Box

Between scuffed balls, spitballs, and wicked curves that buckle knees, it ain't easy being a man with a bat trying to do nothing more than make contact, put the ball in play, and help out the team. The thing about breaking pitches, at least the good ones, is that they break late, fooling the batter into thinking that the trajectory they're following will be consistent into the catcher's glove. Of course, if you swing before the pitch breaks, you have a better chance at connecting. So imagine Mariner manager Maury Wills' surprise when, against the A's in 1980, with breaking-ball pitcher Rick Langford going for Oakland, opposing manager Billy Martin pointed out to umps that Seattle's batter's box was one foot over league regulations, and that the extra space was closest to the mound. Wills was "shocked and dumbfounded." He was also suspended for two games and fined $500.

Mission Impossible

Albert Belle was neither the first nor the last batter to be accused of using an unapproved bat. Belle sits comfortably in a long line of would-be sluggers with carpentry aspirations, including Norm Cash, the Tigers first baseman who, after he retired, confessed to using a bat filled with glue, cork, and sawdust; Graig Nettles, the Yankee third baseman, whose broken bat let loose a half-dozen Super balls in a game against the Tigers; and, of course,

Man, that bat was loaded.

George Brett, whose pine-tar-covered bat provided great controversy and legendary highlight footage after Yankee manager Billy Martin waited until Brett hit a home run to point it out to umpires—taking the runs off the board, ruling Brett out, and producing one of the greatest tantrums ever filmed.

Belle stands out on this list for what happened after suspicions were raised in a 1994 game against the White Sox.

Belle's bat was confiscated for inspection after the game, but he and his teammates were all too aware of the cork inside it, and the effect it would have on Cleveland's lineup during a pennant race if their best hitter was suspended for an extended period.

Jason Grimsley volunteered for a mission that would hopefully help save the Tribe's season, agreeing to use a hatch in the ceiling to gain access to a crawl space connecting the clubhouse to the umpire's locker room. After wriggling on his stomach with a flashlight in his mouth for about a hundred feet, Grimsley reached his destination and dropped down on top of a refrigerator. He grabbed Belle's confiscated bat to make the switch, but since all of Belle's bats had been "modified," the only cork-free substitute available was a "Paul Sorrento" model.

When the umpires arrived later and saw that the bat in their possession was no longer Belle's, controversy erupted. (Some say there were even threats made of criminal complaints and FBI involvement.) To avoid a team penalty, Grimsley confessed. He received no punishment, but Belle was suspended for ten games (later reduced to seven). The season-shortening players' strike ensured that the incident would have no effect on the Indians' playoff run.

CHARACTERS, ODDBALLS,
AND PRANKSTERS

One hundred and sixty-two games a season, postseason play, day/night doubleheaders, and a life on the road make for a lot of downtime. And the sport's unique personalities fill all this time in the most peculiar ways. Some do what they do for laughs, while others are just trying to get a win any way they can.

Some Players Get Hot . . .
Others, Not So Much

Sometimes getting a job done right requires an incredible amount of dedication and commitment. Say, for instance, you've taken it upon yourself to scare a teammate into therapy. A slacker might hide something unsavory in the teammate's locker, maybe a spider or a snake. A professional on the other hand, such as '70s

41

Jim Rooker: DNP, Freezer Burn.

pitcher Jim Rooker, understood exactly the amount of work needed to deliver an authentic scare. As it does for many, Rooker saw to his task by getting to work early, which meant arriving at the Pirates' clubhouse first and giving himself enough time to empty one of the refrigerators. He then carefully positioned himself inside the fridge (providing himself with an airway to breathe through) and waited. Some time later, thirsty outfielder John Milner arrived at the clubhouse. As Milner opened the fridge, Rooker lunged, grabbed his arm with icy hands, and screamed. Mission accomplished.

A Horse of a Different Color

In the early '60s, pitcher Mudcat Grant, then with the Cleveland Indians, found himself having an issue with a particular umpire. Grant observed that the ump in question was working third base during the first game of a late-August doubleheader, so he rightfully assumed that he would be behind home plate for the night-cap—the game Grant was scheduled to start. To teach a lesson, Grant recruited his catcher, Joe Azcue, and in his own words, "something that the horses [used for ballpark security] left on the ground." After securing manager Birdie Tebbetts' approval, Grant applied horse manure to the back of Azcue's helmet so that when the umpire leaned in to call balls and strikes, he'd be sure to get a strong whiff. According to Grant, the umpire got further and further back from the plate trying to escape the smell, and in the end, his only recourse was to call strikes. "It was the quickest game I pitched," Grant recalled, "because every pitch . . . 'Strike.' I pitched a game in an hour and thirty-six minutes!"

Minor League Mash

Dave Bresnahan, a catcher and lifetime minor leaguer, was playing for the Williamsport Bills of the Eastern League when, during a game in 1987 against the Reading Phillies, he let loose a pickoff throw to third base that sailed over the infielder's head. The runner on third saw the white sphere bounce into the outfield and immediately took off for home, only to be greeted by Bresnahan with the ball and a smile. He had held on to the ball the entire time, fooling everyone by throwing a peeled potato, the remains of which now littered the grass. Wasting food cost Bresnahan a $50 fine, and a day later, his job. The story did earn the catcher a place in history, as the potato has been preserved in alcohol and is now among the many baseball artifacts found in the Baseball Reliquary's collection in Monrovia, California.

Humble Pie

Every player lives for the moment when they can come through for their teammates and be the man that makes the difference in securing a victory. Pats on the back, high fives, perhaps a *SportsCenter* highlight—those are

I believe I'm one of the best players on the arghumphphoo.

all icing on the cake. Of course, too much icing gets you a stomachache, and there's always a risk that those in-game heroics can go to a guy's head.

The Chicago White Sox have a recipe to keep their teammates humble (two, if you count Ozzie Guillen's tirades), in the form of a whipped-cream pie delivered to the face during post-game interviews (occasionally substituted with shaving cream for the calorie conscious). The Chi-Sox certainly aren't the only team partial to messy desserts, but the 2008 crew developed a reputation for serving up the vaudeville-inspired course on their way to the American League Central title. What started in the spirit of fun and games almost took a turn for the worse when backup catcher Toby Hall tweaked his injured right shoulder while trying to get teammate Jermaine Dye after a 13-5 win over Seattle. With his shoulder wrapped in ice, Hall insisted he was fine, and thankfully he did not need to spend time on the disabled list with a pie-related injury.

Taking the Game Home with You

Reggie Willets lives baseball. So does his family. While coming up through the minors, Willets, his wife Amber, and their son, Jaxon, lived inside an indoor batting cage. What started out as the first structure built in a project that was intended to include a two-story house with a view of the lake, became a solution to the family's need to save money while Willets rose through the ranks, as well as a training tool that could not be denied. The 60 by 30-foot structure housed the family from 2003 through the 2007 season. During that time, Willets improved his swing at home with the help of his wife, who when not busy taking care of the family, would keep the pitching machine churning with practice balls.

With a net suspended from the ceiling to contain the barrage of line drives that would otherwise rip through the "living room" during a good session, Reggie still occasionally needed to rearrange the furniture to access his indoor field. Profiled in a 2007 *New York Times* article by Lee Jenkins, Mrs. Willets was asked what she would look forward to most on the day they moved out of the cage and into their completed home. Her response: the walls.

Home schooling paid off, as Reggie made the Angels opening-day roster in 2007, batting a hair under .300 as a leadoff hitter and finishing in the top five for Rookie of the Year. The 2008 season wasn't as successful for Willets, but what remains to be determined is if his sophomore slump was due to spending too much time at home, or not enough.

The Mayor

When Sean Casey was playing in the Cape Cod League in 1994, he developed a reputation for talking with everyone. The opposing team's runners, announcers, fans, and concession guys all found themselves in conversations with the affable first baseman. His coach at the time teased him about it, asking, "Hey Casey, you lobbying for votes? You running for office?" His nickname, The Mayor, stuck. From idle chit-chat to in-depth conversations about the game he loves, The Mayor is one of the most popular players in the game today. He was even voted "Friendliest Guy in Baseball" in a *Sports Illustrated* poll among 460 of his fellow players.

Once while touring Washington DC, he and his teammates ran into an armed security guard who was wary of their presence until Casey charmed their way past him. Curtis Granderson, the Tigers' center fielder at the time, remembered the incident not only for the instant bond The Mayor created, but also for the group of tourists behind them, whispering among themselves that they knew Casey, having been on the receiving end of his hospitality a few years ago.

Congratulating your opponent for a solid base hit doesn't usually go over well with your pitchers. But as teammate and close friend, Jason Grill reasons, "He understands this is a platform to reach beyond himself."

Still, whether intentional or not, there is some advantage in having a talkative first baseman. Catcher Brandon Inge recalls a conversation with an opposing team's third-base coach who lamented that, "Casey was talking so much that my players weren't paying attention to my signs."

A Team That Brings Tears to Your Eyes

The Kansas City Royals haven't been viewed by anyone as a dangerous team since the George Brett heyday of the early 1980s. In fact, thirteen of their past fourteen seasons ended with losing records. (Their banner year being 2003, with the team finishing 83-79.) So, coming into the All-Star break at 38-50, 2007 had the potential to be another rough one. After losing three of four to the Yankees in late July, KC had just taken the opener in a three-game set against Texas when things got a little rougher.

Following the 6-1 win, KNBC reporter Karen Kornacki was conducting a postgame interview with shortstop Tony Pena, Jr. when the perils of Kansas City became all too apparent as the reporter was accidentally shot in the face with a pellet gun. The marksman was Kansas City outfielder Emil Brown, who was sincerely apologetic for the unintended shooting. (He had been playing with a toy gun when it accidentally discharged.) Fortunately, Kornacki wasn't seriously hurt, though she did have to endure watching the Royals finish out the season. To the team's credit, they broke their streak of consecutive seasons with 100 or more defeats, losing only 87 games and finishing a game out of the cellar and above the Tigers.

Pack Your Bags

For Kyle Kendrick, it began as a normal spring training morning, until he was called into his manager's office. There waiting for him was Charlie Manuel and the Phillies' assistant general manager Ruben Amaro, informing him that he had been traded to the Yomiuri Giants for right-handed pitcher Kobayashi Iwamura. The right-handed pitcher was stunned as he read the official letter from his team detailing the transaction that would send him halfway around the world, especially considering that he had finished the 2007 season with an ERA below 4.00. In a daze and absently clutching the plane ticket that the team had provided him, he made his way around the clubhouse, receiving congratulatory wishes and stunned reaction from his teammates. Fellow pitcher Brett Myers couldn't believe it, though he hoped Kobayashi had a good sinker.

Kendrick's flight didn't leave until the following morning, but first, there was the media to deal with, as a press conference had been scheduled. When asked his thoughts on the deal, all he could do is ask, "Do they have good food in Japan?" There was no follow-up question in response, only Myers' laughter, as he proudly declared to Kendrick, "You got 'punked!'"

Not only were his team's manager, assistant general

manager, and traveling secretary in on Myers' prank, but so were all his teammates, his agent, and the press. The trade documents were faked, as was his ticket. Kobayashi Iwamura wasn't even a pitcher, but rather a reference to the world hot dog eating champion. To top it all off, the whole prank had been recorded, and it's circulating today thanks to the miracle of YouTube.

Hi, This is Adam from Milwaukee . . .

These days there are many voices providing baseball's soundtrack, with three-men booths, studio analysts, and sports talk-radio callers combining to create a symphony of exceptional commentary and awful clamoring. Cincinnati sports host Marty Brenneman has heard it all, so it was no surprise when "Adam from Milwaukee" called in with the standard run of wasted-breath questions.

Adam wanted to know whether or not Brenneman

thought Cincinnati first baseman Scott Hatteberg was a good player. Marty thought he was. Adam thought he was overrated. Adam wanted to see Luke Stowe at first instead. Adam wondered whether it's still raining in Milwaukee. Adam also wanted to know if Marty had his shirt on. . . . Huh?

Adam happened to be Adam Dunn, Cincinnati's starting left fielder. The call took place from inside the clubhouse as Dunn and the Reds waited out a rain delay during the summer of 2006. And while Hatteberg *was* eventually moved for a rookie first baseman, it wasn't Luke Stowe—Stowe was the infant son of one of the Reds' equipment managers.

For the Birds

In 1918, Casey Stengel was traded from the Dodgers to Pittsburgh. With the Pirates playing in Brook-

A tad late for Alfred Hitchcock's casting call.

lyn, Stengel found himself (for the first time) on the wrong end of an Ebbets Field crowd. As the story goes, while playing the outfield, Casey saw a sparrow fly into a wall and crash to the ground. Thinking fast, Stengel picked up the bird and brought it back to the dugout. When his turn to bat came up in the top half of the next inning, the crowd was still giving him a hard time, when he turned, smiled, and doffed his cap—effectively giving the bird back to Brooklyn as the sparrow flew away. (Another version of the story suggests that a friend was nursing the sparrow and Casey "borrowed it.")

Casey's bird encounter had a much happier ending than Dave Winfield's. Winfield was with the Yankees in Toronto in 1983, warming up between innings in the outfield, when an aggressive seagull began swooping down toward him. Trying to scare the bird away, the future hall of famer threw a ball in its general direction, hitting the creature in the neck and killing it instantly. Yankee manager Billy Martin quipped, "That was the first time he hit the cutoff man all season."

Of course, Winfield's bird stood a fighting chance.

During a Giants-Diamondbacks preseason game in 2001, a dove had the misfortune of flying into the path of a Randy Johnson fastball. The highlight clip revealed only an explosion of feathers, as Johnson had recorded one of the messiest outs on record.

OUT OF LEFT FIELD

Not every great play happens on the field . . . or between players. And, in a game measured and relived in numbers and statistics, every now and then, the one-in-a-billion odds come through. When it happens, all you can do is tip your cap.

The Shortstop Gets the Save

A year after being traded by the Red Sox to the Cubs, Boston fan favorite Nomar Garciaparra made the sort of play that would ensure his place in the hearts of Beantown rooters. Although traded during the Red Sox '04 championship campaign, Nomar kept a condominium in Boston.

The all-star shortstop had returned home following the end of Chicago's 2005 season, when late one night he heard a splash and screams from outside his window. Two women had fallen into the harbor, one hitting her head in the process. Nomar and his uncle Victor jumped into the harbor and rescued the women. A witness to the action called the play-by-play by declaring, "It was crazy. Nomar was like jumping over walls to get to the girls, and the other guy leaped off the balcony. It was unbelievable." When one of the two women regained consciousness, her only reaction was to ask her savior, "Are you Nomar?"

Just another diving grab.

Taking the Kiss-Cam Too Far

When Toronto's Rogers Center was first built (then called the Sky Dome), it was the first major-league baseball stadium with a fully retractable-roof. The construction of the tallest and most massive home field in baseball was such an impressive undertaking that time-lapsed video of the process ran on a loop at the Hall of Fame museum in Cooperstown, New York. Blue Jays fans were also treated to a hotel in center field, with rooms that overlooked the field. This feature has provided several crowds with an awkward sideshow over the years, as varied hotel guests have found themselves unaware (or unconcerned) that the windows of their room were not made of one-way glass. Since the park opened in 1989, three couples have found themselves at the center of a stir when their affections found an audience . . . of 50,000. Since the first incident in 1990,

Home run!

Toronto has thankfully seen more exciting action on the field, topped by Joe Carter's walk-off World Series winning home run in 1993—a spectacle that kept the love in the stands and all eyes on the game.

The $100,000 Millionaire

In 2008, when Barry Bonds' marketing agent established the "Million Dollar Arm Hunt," an Indian contest looking for major-league talent among the 1.1 billion residents of the sub-continent, Indian javelin thrower, Rinku Singh's 87 mph fastball took home the prize. (Baseball's exchange rate being what it is, a million-dollar arm only paid out $100,000.) Major-league scout Ray Poitevint took a flight out to see if a game-show winner could make it in the big show, and came away thinking that Singh, along with Dinesh Patel (also a javelin thrower), a harder thrower with some control issues, could both be worth a look. Singh and Patel had never seen a live baseball game before. They learned how to speak English by watching *Baseball Tonight*, were mystified by delivery pizza, and still had some questions about the game. (Patel once asked,

"What did the shortstop do wrong to be the only infielder without a base?") These Indians both had strong arms from years of field-event training, and after working with acclaimed pitching coach Tom House, they earned an audition in front of twenty major-league clubs. And you couldn't imagine a happier Hollywood ending, as Pittsburgh signed them both to minor-league deals.

Magical
Stuff

FOR over half of the calendar year, the game of baseball is as steady a factor in the lives of its fans as the sunrise. The sport is a part of most every day, and as its eventual setting is marked with the last out, all that remains is the promise of another game tomorrow. The seasons pass with a similar cadence, with each change in weather linked to a phase of the game. And for all but one team, each campaign ends with nothing more than a call to next year to redeem or relive the respective sins and glories of the past. Many a morning mood has been soured by an extra-inning loss the night before; many a winter holiday has had some extra cheer thanks to eleven October wins.

It should be no surprise then that such a presence takes on a life of its own. A complicated system of superstitions and rites emerges for every devoted follower looking to control what they cannot. From inside-out rally caps to lucky spots on the couch, we believe that something beyond the nine men on the field and the one up to bat will affect the outcome. Players are no different. Keith Hernandez often tells the story of his vantage point for the New York Mets' two-out, 10th-inning rally in Game 6 of the 1986 World Series—sitting in manager Davey Johnson's office watching the game on television. When asked why he didn't leave his seat to return to the dugout, Hernandez responded, "That chair had more hits in it."

Derek Jeter often invoked the ghosts of old Yankee Stadium. (He wasn't the first to do so.) During the 2001 World Series, Curt Schilling learned the hard way what happens when you rub a ghost the wrong way. Schilling referred to the stadium's "mystique" and "aura" as "dancers in a nightclub," only to have his Diamondbacks lose

Hey! Babe Ruth's ghost just ate all the hot dogs!

back-to-back games due to late-inning Yankee home runs. One of them was Jeter's famous "Mr. November" walk-off shot to win Game 5.

Of course, aura and mystique can only carry a team so far. When the supernatural "fails" to pull the home team out of the fire, when the mojo stops rising, the tomahawk won't chop, and the rally monkey dances his last dance, we're often reminded that the same magic works both ways. If the un-strapping and strapping of batting gloves before a turn at the plate can help a player get a hit, it's only fair that a curse can stand in the way of franchise success for generations. Long after a team's roster has turned over, uniforms and playing fields remain haunted with the identities triggered by a bad hop or an errant throw—the team is cursed.

Curses explain the unexplainable; they are the conspiracy theories that balance out the enormous weight of both the unlucky and the poorly executed. It's not enough that "somebody had to lose," not when years and lifetimes are invested on a team. When loving a team makes us miserable, we want answers. Blame the Billy Goat, the Bambino, even the Devil himself; somebody's got to answer for unearned runs and an inability to hit with runners in scoring position.

If a league full of teams can play over a century's worth of seasons, and we can still regularly see something new, there's probably room for a little magic and mysticism from time to time. What follows are some of the more powerful spells cast, conjured, or imagined by players and fans.

SUPERSTITIONS

Perhaps superstitions in baseball are the supernatural first-response squad that puts out the mystical fires of bad luck before they have the chance to engulf a player or a team in a five-alarm curse. The smaller demons are fed to keep the larger demons at bay.

Tearing Up the Mound

In retrospect, Bobo Newsom may have had an obsessive-compulsive disorder, but at the time, his teammates and friends just assumed he was superstitious. One of Newsom's hang-ups was tied to the state of the pitcher's mound. He wanted it pristine before he pitched. One day before a game that Newsom was scheduled to pitch for Detroit in the late '30s, opposing ace Bob Feller and third baseman Kenny Keltner decided to have a little fun with him. The teammates bought a bag of confetti. Keltner then stuffed his pockets with the colorful pieces of paper, only to empty them later as he walked across the diamond. With the mound covered in confetti right before the scheduled first pitch, Newsom refused to start the game until the grounds crew came out and every last piece was picked up. After a twenty-minute delay, during which the mound was perfectly manicured, the game could finally begin.

The Smell of Success

Ryne Duren had something of a "wild thing" reputation as a pitcher, bringing him success as a reliever with the Yankees in the '60s. He had a hard fastball, a reputation for drinking, a pair of thick "Coke bottle" glasses, and a habit of occasionally throwing warm-up pitches against the backstop to intimidate opposing batters. Duren also had a bit of a superstition. He refused to change the sweatshirt he wore beneath his jersey until he lost a game. In his own words he "lost a lot of friends in the locker room" as a result.

*Me, scared of a little kitty? Naw. I'm allergic . . .
yeah, that's it. Allergic.*

Part Goat, Part Black Cat, All Bad Luck

It looked like 1969 would be a good year for the Cubs.
With a comfortable lead in the newly formed National
League East, they were positioning themselves to play

for their first pennant in fifteen years. As summer came to a close however, the team began to stumble just as the perennial bottom-dwelling Mets showed signs of life for the first time in their franchise history. By early September, the Mets had pulled within a game and a half, and the teams had a pivotal two-game series against each other. During the first game, a black cat jumped onto the field and circled Cubs' third baseman Ron Santo, and then proceeded to pace in front of the Chicago dugout before disappearing into the stands. The Cubs lost the game, and a day later they lost their lead in the standings for good. Years later, Santo told a radio audience that he believed the jinxed feline was no coincidence. According to Santo, Cubs manager Leo Durocher was extremely superstitious, and the Mets were aware of it. Santo claimed Ernie Banks, who was friendly with just about everyone, got it on good authority from the New

York clubhouse that the Mets had brought the cat to the field and let it loose to spook them.

Counter Cursed

When it came to the Senators, Cleveland pitcher Mud-cat Grant was a one-man filibuster, having started his career by winning his first thirteen decisions against the DC club. In response, the Senators hoped to exorcise the mojo working against them and prevent the streak from being extended further. So, in July of 1960, with the Indians in town and Grant scheduled to pitch, Broad-caster Bob Wolff mixed and then drank a "potion" of exotic ingredients during the pregame, black cats were let loose on the field, "natives" were brought in to spread "magic dust" on the mound, and if all else failed, both Miss Maryland and Miss Virginia were on hand to pro-vide distraction. Nine innings later, when the dust had cleared, Cleveland still won the game, Mudcat had his fourteenth consecutive decision and three RBIs against Washington pitcher Camilo Pascual, and Wolff got a stomachache. In retrospect, the rituals might have had a delayed reaction, as two weeks later, Grant pitched a complete game against Washington and lost 3-2.

#99

As the 20th century came to a close, no pitcher came close to Turk Wendell as far as superstitions were concerned. In addition to the standard jumping over the third- and first-base lines whenever he enters or leaves the diamond (Sparky Anderson once did the same, but chose to merely step over the line), Turk has a long list of quirks that gets stranger the further back in his career you look. His major-league eccentricities included spiking the rosin bag each time he used it, which drew approval from his home crowd, while creating a cloud of dust. Early in his career when he played for the Cubs, he would refuse to catch a ball if an umpire threw it back to him. When he came to the Mets, his lucky number 9 was already worn by catcher Todd Hundley. So he took #99 instead. That by itself is tame, but a few years later, when he renewed his contract, he negotiated himself the sum of $9,999,999.99.

As a reliever, whenever Turk was used for longer stretches, he would brush his teeth after each inning. Prompting his excessive brushing were the four sticks of black licorice he chewed each inning he was on the mound. While he chewed, he might be standing or squatting, depending on the upright position of his catcher at the time—if his catcher was up, Turk was down, and vice versa. Not to leave the center fielder out of the mix, Wendell would wave to him at the start of each appearance—a ritual that went back to high school for him, when his best friend played center and the two would acknowledge each other with a wave before Turk got to work.

When asked about it, Wendell admitted to some element of gamesmanship, saying, "If they think I'm weird and that gives me an edge, I'll use it to help my team."

The Chicken Man

While Turk Wendell was certainly one of baseball's most interesting characters, his oddball behavior barely got his lifetime ERA below 4 (3.93). Stan "The Man" Musial (whose career spanned twenty-two seasons beginning in 1941) would occasionally turn to mental trickery to break a slump. (He would disturb his breakfast ritual by eating his cereal and eggs out of order.) And perhaps his perfectly even 1,815 hits both on the road and at home hint at some fondness for order. In recent history, however, it's Wade Boggs who takes the superstition crown. Boggs rode eighteen years of honored and regimented superstitions from 1982 to 1999 to a .328 lifetime batting average and admittance into the Hall of Fame.

For Boggs, it all began in fowl territory with chicken for dinner before every game. Then it was onto the diamond for infield practice, where he would take exactly 150 ground balls. He followed with designated times for entering the batting cage and taking wind sprints. Boggs left the infield by stepping on third base, then second, then first, then the baseline, and then two steps in the coach's box with four steps from there to the dugout. When all is said and done, his checklist was rumored to have included somewhere between sixty and seventy superstitions. At the end of the day, he would see to the last of them by tying his special sanitary socks in a recognizable knot so that the clubhouse manager doing laundry could identify them. Boggs didn't want the socks mixed up with the rest of the team's.

The Rose Goes in the Front, Big Guy

Jason Giambi's secret for busting slumps might make Victoria blush: a gold lamé thong with a flame-lined waistband. More effective than a rabbit's foot or a lucky penny, Giambi has been using the thong to enhance his performance since his days with the Oakland A's during the late '90s—saving the shiny undergarment for those special occasions when he was stuck in the depths of his worst slumps. After signing with the Yankees in 2002, the power of the G-string became well-known throughout the clubhouse and has since been experienced by several of the slugger's New York teammates. According to Giambi, if you're in a slump, "You've got to come and ask for it . . . that's the way it works."

Derek Jeter and Johnny Damon are among the Bronx Bombers' least bashful lingerie models, with Jeter feeling the payoff the one and only time he donned the thong. While the Yankee shortstop did manage to ride his way out of an 0-for-32 stretch with a first-pitch home run, chances are these won't be everyday skivvies for the perennial all-star. Why? He complained that, "It's so uncomfortable running around the bases." While not always worn, Giambi's underwear has been passed around the locker room, leaving one to hope that good luck doesn't fade in the wash.

CURSES

When you talk about curses and baseball, the two teams that immediately come to mind are the Red Sox and the

Cubs. The championship droughts that each team suffered (and in regards to the Cubs, are still enduring), are ripe for paranormal explanations. The haunted history of each of these clubs has so many painful milestones that they will be explored in a later chapter. What follows are the smaller curses—the ones that only time will tell whether they grow in power or become shattered with the perfectly timed crack of a bat.

The Cost of Labor in Montreal

While no one would ever suggest that the Expos earned a curse in their short history, if the game ever endures another work stoppage, one would be wise to keep an eye on their modern-day incarnate, the Nationals. The first player's strike took place in 1981, and as a result of the shortened season, the postseason participants were determined by first and second-half results, which gave the Expos their first playoff berth. The team made it through a divisional round against the Phillies and found themselves alive in the fifth and deciding game of the NLCS against LA, before giving up a go-ahead home run to Rick Monday in the top of the ninth. Over a decade later, the first-place Expos had the best record in baseball (74-40), only to have the strike of 1994 end the season early without a World Series winner for the first time since 1904. Montreal baseball was never the same after that, and as attendance dropped, so did the team's chance of survival north of the border. What labor giveth, labor taketh away.

The Devil Went Down to Tampa

If you mentioned to a Royals fan that *your* team might be cursed as you had not seen the playoffs during its nine-year existence, you might get laughed at. If you complained in Pittsburgh about year after year of futility on the field, losing records, and busted prospects, you might get beaten. Nevertheless, the nasty-do-well Tampa Bay faithful had a valid point when it came to the losing ways of their Rays. Prior to the 2008 season, the only thing the Devil Rays had done successfully was carry the torch that originated with the '62 Mets—as an expansion team unable to associate itself with winning. From their debut year of 1998 through 2007, the D-Rays were unable to put together a winning season, and in fact, once blew sixty leads in a single season (2006).

In 2008, ownership enacted an organization-wide exorcism, with new uniforms, new logos, and a Devil-free Rays team ready to take the field. The new-look Rays were so committed to their reborn identity that if personnel were caught saying the "D-word," they were

Back to New Jersey, where you belong!

charged a dollar (donated to charity). Compelled by the power of their new marketing initiative (not to mention some solid trades and a stocked farm system), the Rays not only had their first winning season, they won the American League pennant and advanced to the World Series. Unfortunately, the Rays failed to shine during a World Series that saw torrential rain and a Philadelphia opponent looking to end a drought of its own.

Cover Boy

Seventies band Dr. Hook & The Medicine Show once sang about getting their picture on the cover of *Rolling Stone* (thanks to lyrics by Shel Silverstein). At one time, some ballplayers may have had similar aspirations about *Sports Illustrated*; at least they did until the notion of an *SI* jinx began to take hold. (Though, going back as far as the 1930s, there was some suggestion of a *Time* sports-related cover jinx, as well). In 2001, *SI* did a study of athletes who had appeared on the cover and then suffered some fall off shortly after. They found 913 occurrences after 2,456 covers. That's a .372 average!

According to *Sports Illustrated*, the legend goes back to their first issue, when Eddie Matthews of the Milwaukee Braves graced the cover. Soon after, his team's nine-game winning streak was snapped, and Matthews missed seven games after getting hit in the hand by a pitch. A decade later, after winning his first four decisions for the Indians with two one-hit shutouts, it was pitcher Sam McDowell featured up front—only to leave his next game in the top of the first having given up five runs while recording no outs, and then lasting an inning and two-thirds in the start after that. Other victims include Nolan Ryan, who lost eight consecutive decisions after his cover, along with sluggers George

I'm finally going places.

Brett, Dale Murphy, Kirk Gibson, Dwight Evans, Barry Bonds, and Mo Vaughn, who each saw a slump or a team losing streak following their appearances. Matt Williams was an early leader in each of the Triple Crown categories on June 5, 1995, when his cover debuted. On June 8th, he broke his right foot after fouling a pitch off it and was out until September. In July 2006, it was the New York Mets on the cover, and while it's hard to suggest that a gut-wrenching, Game 7 loss in the NLCS three months later could have been the result, there's nothing like tempting fate. A year later, the team appeared on the cover again, this time with their general manager. There could be no doubting the results as they blew a seven-game lead in the NL East by going 5-12 down the stretch.

A Yankee Dandy

For years, the only cursing coming out of Yankee Stadium came from the bleachers. Unrivaled franchise success left little room to entertain mystical explanations for the occasional dry spell—the worst of which barely lasted fifteen years. In fact, the opposite has long been suggested, with years of good fortune owing to some unidentified good-luck charm, which was allegedly tossed into the water-main pit before it was graded over by a subcontractor working the original construction site of Yankee Stadium. It's only by reading between the lines (and the championships) that any argument about the occult or otherwise can be made.

In 1981, New York took home the American League pennant, sweeping Oakland in the American League Championship Series only to lose the World Series to the Dodgers in six games after going up 2-0 in the series. The loss was marked by an alleged fight between team owner, George Steinbrenner, and several Dodger fans in an LA elevator. Even so, the loss still marked a successful six-year stretch for the Yankees that included four pennants and two world championships.

The following season, the "Hitman" himself, Don Mattingly made his major-league debut. The lack of a championship over the next twelve seasons, spanning Donnie Baseball's playing career, would be nothing of note if the story ended there. Three elements turn our attention to the possibility of some malevolent magical force hiding behind number 23's mustache. To begin, we look at the '94 and '95 seasons, each of which suggested the Yankees were ready to once again turn the corner. In 1994, the Yankees had the best record in the American League, only to have the player's strike end the season early and cancel the playoffs. In 1995, the Yankees made the playoffs via the wild card, and were up 2-0 against the Mariners before losing three in a row—ending their playoff run and any chance Mattingly would have at playing in a World Series. He retired during the off-season. Following his departure, New York went on its best run since Casey Stengel's teams of the '50s, winning four of the next five championships, back-to-back-to-back from 1998-2000.

Mattingly retained ties to the organization as a spring-training instructor, and returned to the team as a hitting coach in 2004. His homecoming allowed him a field-level view of the greatest postseason collapse in baseball history, as his Yankees coughed up a 3-0 series lead to the rival Red Sox, ending an eighty-six-year Sox curse in the process. The next three postseasons proved disappointing as well, each serving up a one-win, first-round dismissal.

Mattingly left the organization after the 2007 season, and only time will tell whether there was something supernatural at work countering the subterranean charm hidden away over eighty years ago. Of course, if the good-luck power of the charm buried beneath the

With this jersey, I'll cement Boston's legacy!

old stadium is to be believed, then perhaps fans have something to worry about in their new stadium. Gino Castignoli, a Red Sox fan working the site during construction, announced to the world in April 2008 that he had mixed a David Ortiz Red Sox jersey in with the concrete that formed the stadium's foundation. The artifact was quickly unearthed, but about a month later, he revealed that he had also buried a scorecard from the same 2004 ALCS that so miserably ended Mattingly's first season as a hitting coach.

Iron Giants

If the Giants were a cursed team, the catalyst for their misfortune must be due to relocation. After all, the New York Giants packed up their Polo Ground roots and headed west, taking Mays and the rest of the team with them and breaking the hearts of generations of fans in the process. Of course, Walter O'Malley took his team out of Brooklyn on the same cross-country route, and the Dodgers went on to win four pennants and two world championships in their new digs. So if there is a Giant curse, it goes beyond California baseball.

If over fifty years of postseason futility requires an otherworldly explanation, perhaps the answer lies in an unkept promise. When journeyman player Eddie Grant died as a World War I hero, the Giants honored him with a plaque and monument. Resting in fair territory, in the deep center field of the Polo Grounds, the tribute to Captain Edward Leslie Grant was commemorated in 1921 and bore witness to thirty years of golden-era ball. When the Giants announced their move, ownership promised that the plaque would make the trip. However, it was either lost or stolen along the way. Decades passed, and with them the Giants suffered a World Series loss to their former cross-town rival in 1962, the Yankees; another to their cross-bay rivals, the A's in 1989; and a third to another interstate rival, the Angels, in 2002. (The latter happened after allowing a 3-2 series lead slip away with a late-inning, six-run rally in Game 6 and a loss in Game 7. Four years later, a replica plaque was dedicated at AT&T Park.

The Curse of the Colonel

As baseball exports itself around the world, it sends its curses and superstitions beyond its borders, as well. For instance, when the Hanshin Tigers won Japan's championship in 1985, their fans took to heart a rather unique Japanese tradition of jumping in the river to honor players they physically resemble. Going down the lineup, fans took turns throwing themselves into the Dotonbori River. But there was a problem upholding the tradition when it came to star slugger Randy Bass. Bass was an American power hitter who never actually hit for power in the majors, but made out well thanks to a favorable foreign exchange rate. With few Hanshin fans resembling the bearded Oklahoma native, Tigers fans went for the next best thing—a statue of Colonel Sanders in front of a Kentucky Fried Chicken.

Over twenty years passed without another Tiger championship, and fans believed that the missing statue was to blame. While it wasn't quite Babe Ruth's piano (famously and regrettably submerged by Boston fans in the 1920s and recovered prior to the end of their eighty-six-year drought), the statue was found in 2009, and with it, Hanshin had its first fresh bucket of hope of the 21st century.

Painful
Stuff

EVERY fan in Mudville knows the moment well. It starts with hope and grows to certainty. The stars seemingly align as if following a script—if not straight from the baseball gods, then clearly from their creative staff. Eight innings or so of sloppy play and restless action was all prelude to the developing story: the comeback, the walk-off win, the inning of play that redeems everything that preceded it. Maybe it was eight years of leaky bullpens and rally-killing double plays. Maybe it was eighty years, each marked with gut-wrenching errors and bad calls. But none of that matters, because tomorrow's papers will forgive all of yesterday's sins. One base hit and we're even in the loss column . . . one more out and we've won it all. Cue the music that sparks the shivers, and light the firework fuse because the Hollywood ending is a pitch away . . . for the other team.

The mystery team across the diamond from Mudville's team had taken a two-run lead into the ninth. They got two ground ball outs and thought they had it locked up before a Flynn single and Blake double brought the go-ahead run to the plate. Fans of this visiting team will question the legitimacy of the fabled slugger who couldn't get the bat off his shoulder until he was down 0-2—and then flailed wildly at what might have been ball one. While the visitor's celebrate their storybook finish on the mound, Mudville's most bitter will gather and claim that Casey choked, that he's overrated and nowhere near as clutch as he could be. Decades will pass and new generations of Mudville players will carry the weight of Casey's failure until they find success where he failed. The team will be cursed, and the sun will not shine until an as-of-yet unformed Mudville team of nine reclaims the happy ending for the heavy-hearted.

Yo, Casey! Maybe you should CHOKE up on the bat some more.

What follows hurts. Some fan out there cringes at the notion that their franchise low lives on. The basic economics of the game dictate that for a rally to be worth celebrating, it's gotta be painful for someone else.

103

Any team from Tampa can lose the World Series 4-1 after a short history of play and walk away unscathed. But for every Game-7, extra-inning, walk-off single, there's another crate of champagne in Cleveland gaining only in vintage. For every wave of goose bumps that greets Met fans at the recital of Vin Scully's "behind the bag" declaration during the '86 World Series, a bar in Boston observes a moment of silence.

Time may heal all wounds, but what Red Sox fans know and Cubs fan hope to realize is that a World Championship is better than any antibiotic at fighting the infection of failure. (And while we talk about curses elsewhere in this book, the history of Chicago and Boston hardship respectively and respectfully belongs right here.) Almost every team has a gut-wrenching moment or two that haunts its fans.

If the greatest victories must be accompanied by the

most painful defeats, here's the stuff good times are made of.

OF BLUNDERS, GOATS, BLACK CATS, AND BALLS TOO FOUL FOR WORDS

If you believe former Cubs manager Lee Elia, perhaps Cub fans are too fair-weather to feel the pain of years of futility. Elia's infamous 1983 rant suggested (with more beeps than a gridlock alert day) that the friendly confines of Wrigley Field had gotten what they deserved. After 2003, however, even Elia might have suggested that those (censored)-ing (censored)-ers deserved a break. Of course, it's only fitting that the last moment of Cubs' glory came at what must have been an excruciating price for their vanquished rivals for the NL pennant, the Giants. Perhaps they angered the baseball gods in the process and have been suffering their wraith ever since.

The Original Goat

For almost every play that still stings years after the final out, there seems to be a goat—one player or person held accountable by the fans for their team's failure. For the Cubs, there happens to be an actual goat that gets some of the credit. As the story goes, Billy Sianis, a local restaurant owner, attempted to bring his billy goat into the stadium during the 1945 World Series against the Tigers. When he was asked to leave (and to take the animal with him), he cursed the team for the offense. It's a story that gets a lot of play whenever the Cubs break hearts around the friendly confines of Wrigley. Of course, the goat incident occurred nearly forty years into the Cubs' World Series drought. So as far as curses go, it lacks coverage. Some have suggested that the years of regular-season futility following 1945 had as much to do with the Cubs' initial refusal to install lights, which

Get the goat! He's baaaaaaad luck.

forced their players to play more day games after road trips than any other team. Surely then, as night games arrived at Wrigley, and area livestock found better things to do with their time than frequent North Side bars, Chicago was due for a reversal of fortune.

Merkle's Blunder

When the Giants played in New York's Polo Grounds, at the conclusion of each game, players would typically exit through center field, doing so ahead of the crowds that would follow the same route. In 1908, playing the Cubs in September, with both teams in a pennant race, a 1-1 game entered the bottom of the ninth.

With one out and a runner on, Giants outfielder Moose McCormick hit into a fielder's choice and wound up safe at first. The next batter was rookie Fred Merkle, who singled, advancing McCormick to third. It has been reported that Merkle hit the ball hard enough to stretch it to a double. But with two outs and the only run of importance being ahead of him, it was seen as smart baseball to stay put.

What happened next became an instant legend with conflicting stories abound. Al Bridwell hit a hard single, scoring McCormick and sending Giant fans rushing onto the field to celebrate the win and make their way home. Seeing the crowd, Merkle decided to do the same, making straight for center field. The problem was, he never touched second base. What is known for certain is that Cubs second baseman Johnny Evers spotted the miscue. Now, Evers had tried to catch a Pittsburgh base runner doing the same thing a few weeks prior, only the umpire at second, Henry O'Day, admitted to not seeing whether the runner had reached the base. In the game against the Giants, O'Day was behind the plate and alert to the possibility. He confirmed that Merkle had not made it to second. Reports are that Cub center fielder Art Hofman threw the ball in, and that either the play was completed but there was so much confusion on the field that the game could not be continued, or that Giants pitcher Joe McGinnity had intercepted the ball and thrown it into the stands—only to have either the same ball or a substitute eventually returned to the field. Either way, the runner was out and the game would have to be resumed at a later date if it bore weight on the standings.

When both teams finished the season tied for first place, the play, and the game, took on great significance. The Cubs won the "do over" and with it, the pennant. The Giants lost the season on what amounted to a technicality, and Merkle's Blunder was born. The pain here was all New York's, but fortunately they would win three pennants over the next five seasons and take home a title within ten. The Cubs would not be so lucky.

Foul Ball

Ninety-five years after Merkle's Blunder gave the Cubs a pennant, Chicago was five outs away from another (what would have been their first since the infamous goat of '45). Up three games to two with a 3-0 lead in the 8th inning of the 2003 NLCS, things suddenly went horribly wrong. Perhaps the first sign of bad things to come happened a half-inning earlier when comedian Bernie Mac led the crowd in "Take Me Out to the Ball Game" and got a little ahead of himself. He told everyone to, "Root, root, root for the *champions*!" instead of the "home team." The baseball gods took notice. With one out in the eighth and a runner on second, Luis Castillo sent a foul ball down the left-field line that

111

The guys at work will love me if I catch this!

might have been playable for left fielder Moises Alou. Alou reached into the stands just as a fan, unaware of Alou's efforts, reached up for the ball. The fan needed to be escorted from the stands for his own protection after it was assumed he had interfered with the play. (Five years later, in between trips to the DL, Alou admitted that he wouldn't have caught the ball anyway, despite claiming the contrary after the game.) When play resumed, the floodgates opened. First a walk to Castillo, followed by an Ivan Rodriguez single, making the score 3-1. Then Miguel Cabrera hit what should have been an inning-ending double play, only to have shortstop Alex Gonzalez boot it. A Derrek Lee double tied the game, and five more runs would cross the plate before the inning ended. The Cubs never recovered, losing the game and eventually the series.

While Cubs fans are still waiting for their first title in what is now over a century, it's the fan caught in the middle of bad baseball who suffered most. We all say and hope we would have been alert enough to give the home-team fielder room to make the play, but no one gets a ticket to what could be a pennant-clinching game thinking they will leave the stadium a pariah. The ball at the center of the controversy was blown up as part of a publicity stunt to exorcise whatever negative energy might have inhabited it. Maybe they should have taken care of Alex Gonzalez's glove too, just to be safe.

CURSING THE BAMBINO

For many Boston fans, the era of the curse (1918-2004) was most painful when it was suggested that somehow trading Babe Ruth was to blame for their team's misfortune. (And if not the *most* painful, then at least fourth most painful.) The hardest part for many was that the motivation for the Ruth deal was reduced in the telling to being nothing more than Sox owner Harry Frazee's desire to fund his play *No No Nanette.* Whether or not this is the truth hardly seems to matter to devout fans.

Trading Babe

Author Glenn Stout detailed the truth behind the transaction in his book *Yankee Century*. Stout confirmed that Frazee was indeed a theater man, but his motives in the Ruth deal were tied to the politics of the league. First, he was in a feud with AL President Bam Johnson. Second, Frazee was in a dispute over the debts his predecessor left before he took over the team. In fact, his ownership of the team was in jeopardy because he did not own Fenway Park and feared it could be sold to a third party in an attempt to muscle him out. Needing money to protect his interests, and tired of Ruth's antics, Frazee had two options: Trade Ruth to the White Sox for "Shoeless" Joe Jackson and $60,000 in cash or trade him to the Yankees for $100,000. The rest is history. And while the move launched the Yankees' first run at greatness, the logic at the time was sound. That doesn't reverse the four very painful plays that the franchise fans suffered over the next 85 years, but it lays the blame on the distortion of fact more than a curse. Trading Babe Ruth to fund a Broadway musical adds insult to injury. Making a deal to save your franchise is just part of the game.

A Pesky Throw

The pain of Johnny Pesky's throw home is twofold. It starts with the 1946 World Series between the Red Sox and the Cardinals, which at the time of this story, was tied at three games apiece. Game 7 found itself tied 3-3 going into the bottom of the 8th inning. Enos Slaughter was on first with two outs, when Cardinal left fielder Harry Walker stroked a double into left-center field. According to Pesky, Slaughter was stealing second base on the pitch, prompting him, as the shortstop, to cover the bag. After Walker connected, Pesky positioned himself in short left-center as a relay man. Slaughter never stopped running, and for years, Pesky was accused of holding on to the ball for too long as the runner beat his throw home. St. Louis took a lead they would not relinquish.

A Game 7 loss is never easy (and the Sox would have their share) but more than anything, it seems that history made a goat out of Pesky, as footage of the play shows no discernible lag in the throw. Not helping his reputation any was Walker's claim that he tried to fool Pesky into making a throw to second allowing the run to score. But again, footage suggests no such move—only a play that could have been executed better, even if credit should probably go to Slaughter more than anything else. Slaughter agrees, and suggests that a more accurate and timely throw, along with better directions from the Boston infielders as to where the ball needed to be thrown, would only have made the play closer.

The Killer B's Part I: Bucky

The setup is simple enough: 162 games wasn't enough to decide the '78 season in regards to the AL Eastern Division title. The Red Sox had already given back a big lead to the Yankees in the standings, capped with a four-game series sweep by NY in Beantown—forever remembered as the "Boston Massacre." And when all was said and done, a one-game playoff in Boston was required. That game was going in Boston's direction, with the Sox up 2-0 in the seventh. New York had put two runners on, but with light-hitting shortstop Bucky Dent facing Mike Torrez, the matchup definitely seemed tilted in the home team's favor. Dent came through for the Yankees with the unlikeliest of home runs, golfing Torrez's 1-1 offering over the Green Monster and earning himself a new middle name in Boston in the process—one that isn't family friendly but has kept on trucking for over thirty years.

Years later, then-Boston manager Don Zimmer would get a morsel of revenge after coming to New York as Billy Martin's third-base coach. Needing a place to stay, he was offered Dent's, but when he got there he saw pictures of the famous swing featured in almost every room. Zimmer called Dent and told him, "I took your pictures and put them facing the wall!"

The Killer B's Part II: Buckner

The Buckner play in Game 6 of the 1986 World Series has been written about from so many different perspectives that there is little new anyone can bring to the discussion. It is everything ever said about the thrill of victory and the agony of defeat—all tied up into one ball rolling away behind the bag and down the line. If somehow you're staring blankly at the page right now, read on.

On October 7, 1986, Boston first baseman Bill Buckner confessed in an interview with a local TV station that, "The nightmares are that you are going to let the winning run score on a ground ball through your legs." Nineteen days later, the Red Sox were up in the series 3-2 against the Mets and were entrenched in a wild Game 6 at Shea that had already seen New York come back twice to erase different Boston leads.

In extra innings, Dave Henderson had put Boston up with a solo home run. A few batters later, a second run was in, and Buckner was hit by a pitch. This gave Boston manager John McNamara the perfect opening to send in Dave Stapleton as a pinch runner and eventual defensive replacement at first when the Sox took the field—a move McNamara had employed throughout the postseason. This time, however, he chose to keep Buckner in so he could be on the field for the eventual victory celebration. (After all, even the Shea scoreboard was congratulating Boston on their win.) However, the Mets' hitters didn't get the memo as Gary Carter, Kevin Mitchell, and Ray Knight all got hits off former Met Calvin Schiraldi—all after Schiraldi had recorded two outs. Knight's hit brought the Mets within one. In response, McNamara brought in reliever Bob Stanley to face speedy outfielder Mookie Wilson. Before working a full count on Wilson, Stanley had uncorked a wild pitch, tying the game and putting the winning run in scoring position.

What followed was a routine slow ground ball, and perhaps even a first baseman whose ankles weren't as

Oopsy. There go my endorsement deals.

achy as Buckner's would have had a hard time getting Wilson at first. But the ball got by Buckner, and Knight scored from second—game over. And with the series tied at three, the momentum shift was obvious. Buckner was the goat, more than Torrez and Pesky ever were, as the play overshadowed his career and became his legacy. More than that, across New England, parents had woken up their sleeping children with two outs in the 10th so that they could see the Sox finally win one—just as kids in New York were trying to stay awake and hold on to the notion that if you want something to happen badly enough, it will happen. For one to cheer, the other had to cry, which, when all is said and done, is why the game is played.

The Killer B's Part III: Boone

Perhaps this was the game that, more than any other, gave the talk of a curse a life of its own. It was another Game 7, another close game, and yet one more chance to beat the Yankees. Pulling out the 2003 ALCS would not have been a guarantee of greater things to come, but defying the inevitability that seemed to envelop every New York/Boston match-up would have gone a long way. Meanwhile, succumbing to the inevitable would only make New York's hold over Boston fans that much stronger.

The series had been a back-and-forth affair, with Boston winning the first game, New York winning the next two, Boston tying up the series, New York pulling ahead, and Boston rallying in Game 6 to force Game 7. All throughout the contest, emotions ran high, including a bench-clearing brawl in Game 3 after starting pitchers Roger Clemens and Pedro Martinez experienced some "control problems." (The most memorable moment of the altercation was Yankee bench coach Don Zimmer charging Pedro, the latter throwing the former to the ground.)

Game 7 was played at Yankee Stadium, and even

though the Sox had jumped out to an early lead, no one thought the game would end quietly. A pair of Jason Giambi solo home runs brought New York back into the game. And then in the eighth, a Bernie Williams RBI and a Jorge Posada two-run double tied it all up. The game went to extra innings . . . of course.

Aaron Boone had come to the Yankees in a late-season trade. He hit a hair above .250 with a half-dozen home runs, but was pretty much a forgotten man in the series with only two hits to his credit. It's safe to say that with Tim Wakefield on the mound—a pitcher whose knuckleball had baffled Yankee hitters all season—no one thought Boone had a game-winning homer in him. (Hmm . . . sound familiar?) He was the easy out that needed to be put down quickly before the top of the order came back around. With his older brother in the broadcast booth, Boone sent the first pitch he saw from

Wakefield over the left-field fence. Another painful chapter for Sox fans, even as history would show that it was merely the darkest hour before the dawn.

MEET THE MESS

Following the amazing success of the Mets' 1986 team and the stunning upset at the hands of the Dodgers in 1988, New York's National League team entered a decade-long downward spiral that, on its own, was no worse than the rebuilding years of any other franchise. The twisting of the blade didn't begin until their AL counterparts began their run in 1996. New York is not the only two-team city in the game, and while Cubs' fans watched the White Sox celebrate on the south side, and the Giants have not only heard the cheers from the A's across the bay but also listened at their own expense, no team in recent memory has had to sit backseat to a dynasty in their own yard. Of course, sitting in a stew of envy only makes things worse.

Dead Man's Hand

What realignment took away from the Mets' realistic postseason chances, the wild card gave right back. Atlanta's own postseason run atop the NL East would extend for fourteen years, but in the wild card there was a chance to at least sniff the rarified air.

New York's first crack at October baseball came in 1998. With five games left in the season, they were in the race with a one-game lead over the Cubs and a three-game lead over San Francisco. A single win would have at least tied them with the other two clubs. They lost all five. Across town, the Yankees would win it all.

The next year would see a baby-step's worth of improvement. After a brief September swoon, the team found itself down one game with three to play. They swept a three-game series against Pittsburgh, beat Cincinnati in a one-game playoff, and then cruised passed the Diamondbacks in the NLDS. Facing the Braves in the NLCS, they stumbled out of the gate and lost the first three games. Before the Red Sox found themselves in the same spot five years later, climbing out of an 0-3 hole was still in the realm of the impossible. But there was hope after a marathon Game 5 that ended on Robin Ventura's grand-slam single. (Ventura cleared the wall with the bases loaded in extra innings, but before he could touch all the bases he was mobbed by teammates.) Game 6 brought the series back to Atlanta, and after falling into another early hole, the Mets fought back. There was hope, destiny, and magic in the air . . . until pitcher Kenny Rogers walked in the series-clinching run for Atlanta with the bases loaded. Across town, the

Yankees would win it all . . . again.

Subway Derailed, Blood on the Tracks

For sure, 2000 would be the year. The regular season ended with some disappointment. Another swoon knocked the Mets out of the NL East race, but for the first time in over a decade, the playoffs came easily, via the wild card. Meanwhile, it was the Yankees who stumbled to the finish line, going 3-15 down the stretch and barely clinging to their division title. With two quick playoff rounds, the Mets returned to the World Series against their cross-town rival, with a chance to erase their second-class status and retake the town.

Game One pretty much summed up the whole series. Up 3-2 in the bottom of the ninth with one out, the Yankees' Paul O'Neal stared down Armando Benitez for a ten-pitch at bat, drew the walk, and scored three batters later. Three innings later, the Yankees won. The next day, Roger Clemens, in an undiagnosed rage, threw a shard of bat at Met catcher Mike Piazza and the Yankees won. (Piazza had owned Clemens until earlier that same season when the Rocket put one in his ear.) Following a John Franco win from a Rick Reed start for the Mets in Game 3, the Yankees took the next two and danced on Shea Stadium's pitchers mound.

The Greatest Meaningless Catch

The World Series loss brought on another team spiral, but by 2006 things had finally changed for the better. A new class of young players, led by David Wright and Jose Reyes, along with the key free-agent signings of Carlos Beltran and Pedro Martinez, produced the most dominant regular season at Shea since '86. After sweeping the Dodgers in the NLDS, the Mets drew the Cards again for the League Championship Series—the same team they beat on the way to their last World Series.

Six games of back and forth baseball left everything knotted up for Game 7 in New York. The game was tied at one run apiece from the second inning on, until Yadier Molina's ninth-inning home run off Aaron Heilman broke the tie game in St. Louis' favor. It was only an inning earlier that Shea was literally rocking. (The upper deck of the old stadium had a tendency to shake when the crowd really got into a game.) Met left fielder Endy Chavez had made a leaping, over-the-wall grab to preserve the tie by taking a home run away from Scott Rolen, and then followed it up by alertly firing the ball to the infield to double Jim Edmonds off first base. Even after Molina silenced the crowd, New York rallied to load the bases in the bottom of the ninth, bringing the team to within a base hit of at least tying the game again. But they came

Look at this lollipop! I'm gonna crush it. I can't wait to swing at this. I'll be a hero. Hey!? Where'd it go?

up short as Carlos Beltran struck out looking at a looping curveball from St. Louis closer Adam Wainwright. There are probably plenty of Mets fans still shaking their heads over this one. But the fun is just beginning.

The Collapse

For the 2007 Mets, the symptoms started weeks before the deathblow. Just as Red Sox fans will forever curse the invocation of Bucky and Boone (and unfairly, Buckner), it should come as no surprise that, moving forward, a generation of Mets fans will suffer an involuntary shutter at the mention of the '07 collapse. After being up seven games with only seventeen to play, New York went into a 5-12 tailspin that was only made worse by the surging play of their I-95 rivals in Philadelphia. This resulted in the two teams being even on the final day of the season. Playing the Marlins with their "ace" on the mound, the Mets had a fighting chance of erasing their stumbling finish and advancing. That chance lasted one-third of an inning when Tom Glavine was pulled from the mound after allowing seven runs while only recording one out. Meanwhile, Philadelphia completed their come-from-behind rally in the standings with a win over Washington. Ironically, it was Philadelphia that had previously held the low watermark for a blown division lead—a detail that the Mets' new nemesis (and natural rival in terms of geography) would never let them forget.

Tearing Down the House

A year later, the 2008 team broke no new ground in again being alive for a playoff spot on the last day of the season. The '08 squad didn't inspire the highest hopes in its followers as it was. At the midway point in the season, controversy surrounded its management, injuries plagued its outfield, and mediocrity overshadowed its play. Then the team got hot, and once again, with seventeen games to go, they found themselves in first place. (This time with less than half the lead.) Bullpen woes ensured that their divisional lead didn't make it to the end of the season, but their playoff hopes remained alive when, with one game to play, they found themselves tied with the Brewers for the wild card.

Upping the stakes, 2008 was the last year of Shea Stadium, and team officials had scheduled a postgame celebration to follow the final regular season home game, with dignitaries from across the franchise's history in attendance.

With the table set for an all-stars-on-deck victory party (and a partial vindication of the previous year's disaster), the Mets battled the Marlins again in game #162. This time it was a tight game that was tied going into the 8th inning. That's when their flailing (and failing) relief corps brought the corpse to the party by giving up back-to-back home runs. Another year, another inning short. Four months later the stadium, and the bullpen, would be dismantled in hopes of a new beginning.

OTHER CUTS FROM THE DIAMOND

Lest we fail to give proper due where it's deserved, here are some other recent sufferers—products of the pain that only our national game can deliver.

Walking the Plank

As hard as it is to remember, in the early '90s Pittsburgh fielded a force to be reckoned with. Led by Jim Leland, anchored by ace pitchers Doug Drabek and John Smiley, and featuring the scaled-down version of Barry Bonds, the Pirates took the NL East crown in 1990, 1991, and 1992.

The 1990 team lost the Championship series to Lou Piniella's Reds, 4-2. In '91, it was the Braves, riding the arm of John Smoltz to a Game 7 victory and the NL pennant. The next year gave Pittsburgh a rematch with Atlanta, and again the series went seven. The Pirates were up 2-0 on the road, with Drabek on the mound in the bottom of the ninth inning. Drabek put the first three batters on, giving up a double to Terry Pendleton, a walk to Sid Bream, with David Justice reaching on an error in between. Reliever Stan Belinda gave up a sacrifice fly to Ron Gant, making the score 2-1, and followed with a walk to Damon Berryhill that reloaded the bases. A pop fly to Brian Hunter put two outs on the board, creating the moment that would see Pittsburgh's last act on a championship stage for quite some time.

With light-hitting Francisco Cabrera up as a pinch hitter, Pittsburgh center fielder Andy Van Slyke reportedly motioned for Barry Bonds to play in a little. Bonds refused. Cabrera put a bloop base hit into play, scoring Justice easily and sending the slow-footed Bream chugging from second on a mad dash home. A gold-glover in left field, Bonds fired a laser beam home. Bream, who by all rights should have been nailed by the on-target throw, was called safe. The series once again went to Atlanta, and with the likes of Bonds and Drabek no longer in the Pittsburgh mix, the team dropped to 5th place the next season and has yet to return to north of .500 play.

Cleveland Rocked

In the discussion of championship droughts, Cleveland is the forgotten city. While the Cubs may still be living in exile of the promised land, Chicago has seen its share of titles from the Bulls, as well as the dominance of the Bears in 1985. The last time "The Cleve" saw a title in one of the four major men's sports (baseball, basketball, football, and hockey) was the 1964 Browns. The last World Series win to go to the Tribe was 1948. Since then they have lost two franchises (the Barons came and went in hockey, the Browns went and came back)

138

and raised no title banners.

In 1997, the Indians were poised to end the city's suffering. After finally getting past the Yankees in the playoffs, Cleveland faced off against expansion-team Florida in the World Series. Neither team could take back-to-back games, sending the series to Game 7 in Florida. Up 2-1 in the bottom of the ninth, Cleveland's Jose Mesa put runners on first and third with one out before being relieved by Gregg Zaun. Craig Counsell lined out to left, but it was enough to sacrifice Moises Alou home and tie the game.

With two outs in the bottom of the 11th, and the bases loaded for Florida, Edgar Renteria singled to the left side of the infield and scored Counsell, giving Florida their first championship in franchise history (five seasons deep), and Cleveland another year without a title.

ONLY FLESH WOUNDS

Not every pain is suffered by a city. Sometimes the wear and tear of the game takes a toll on its players in the most unsuspecting ways. With so much baseball-induced misery providing the foundation for other team's championships, it's safe to say that the best pain is the type that serves others. Let the agony of defeat be balanced by the guilty pleasure of oddball injuries.

Once Bitten

Clarence Blethen was a career minor leaguer who got a big-league call-up with the Red Sox in 1923 (and a second trip with Brooklyn in '29). As a rookie, Blethen got it in his head that a toothless pitcher was somehow more intimidating (or at least looking older) than one with a natural bite, so he got in the habit of removing his artificial choppers and keeping them in his back pocket while he was on the mound. While playing the Tigers, Blethen had, what was for him, a rare base-running opportunity. Standing on first, the rookie reliever took off for second on a ground ball to short, and slid hard into the bag. It was then that he was rudely reminded of the set of teeth not so safely tucked into his uniform, as he effectively bit his own butt.

Dream Warriors

When Jose Cardenal slept, he did so with one eye open. The Cubs outfielder had a history of insomnia, having once complained to manager Whitey Lockman that crickets had kept him up all night and as a result he couldn't play. In 1974, Cardenal had to bow out of opening day because he had slept poorly and one of his eyelids was stuck shut.

Almost thirty years later, the sandman struck again,

this time visiting Glenallen Hill, whose nightmares brought on some real pain. The outfielder had a bad dream about spiders and smashed a glass table near his bed in a panic, cutting up his hands in the process.

All In

As a pitcher in the '70s, Steve Stone had a respectable career. He knew his stuff wasn't dominant enough to make him a superstar, but he had a proverbial ace in the hole to fall back on: a wicked curve. The problem was, throwing it repeatedly would damage his arm.

Stone decided to leave it all on the field for the 1980 Season. Relying heavily on his curve ball, Stone secured his only all-star appearance and went on to lead the league in wins with twenty-five, taking home the Cy Young award. By his own account, "I knew it would ruin my arm. But one year of 25-7 is worth five of 15-

15." He would go 4-7 in '81, his final season on the mound, before moving to the booth where he called games alongside legendary broadcaster Harry Carey. He can currently be seen on the White Sox telecast.

Outrunning the Rain

Vince Coleman was known for his speed, with over 100 stolen bases in each of his first three seasons. A career-high 110 bags swiped during his rookie season helped clear a path for the Cardinals straight to the playoffs. Down 2-0 to the Dodgers, the Cards hoped that when the series returned to Busch Stadium they could ride a home-field advantage to a comeback. Game 3 went to St. Louis, and all that stood in the way of the Cards and a chance to tie the series up, was the weather.

As a light rain fell on the home field's Astroturf surface, the St. Louis grounds crew sprung to life, preparing the mechanized tarp for action. Coleman was on the field stretching, and neither he, nor the grounds crew saw each other until it was too late. Nearly a ton of tarpaulin rolled up on Coleman's leg, trapping the speedster as he screamed for help. It took a half-dozen guys to free him, but with a bone chip in his knee, he was done for the series and the season. Fortunately for the Cards, the rain stopped, and they went on to take the series and eventually, a world championship.

The Constant Gardener

Bobby Ojeda had a good thing going in New York. He was traded to the Mets in time to have an impact on the 1986 World Series. Two years later, Ojeda was again looked upon as a key piece in New York's postseason rotational puzzle. Unfortunately, as the 1988 NLCS against the Dodgers rolled around, Ojeda decided his garden needed some work before the end of the season. On the same day that the Mets clinched a tie for the NL East division title, Ojeda flashed an omen for their ultimate fate that season by nearly severing his middle finger with an electric hedge clipper. Trimming the honeysuckle bushes might have been a "honey-do" chore worth putting off until the offseason, as the Mets were without his 2.88 ERA for the playoffs.

Knocking Boots

Like all major leaguers, Wade Boggs put his pants on one leg at a time. The problem for Boggs came when he put his boots on afterward. In Toronto, with the Red Sox during the 1986 season, the twelve-time all-star and hall of famer lost his balance while putting on his favorite pair of cowboy boots. Boggs took a spill and fell into the hotel's couch, bruising his ribs and kicking himself out of a start in the process.

Boggs' wardrobe mishap came during a bad week for ballplayers and their footwear. Within days of the hotel room spill, two-time all-star Mickey Tettleton went on the disabled list with a foot infection. Apparently, the A's catcher was tying his shoelaces too tightly.

Of course, the patron saint of freak footwear occurrences is Lefty Gomez. The hall-of-fame Yankee pitcher once knocked himself out of a game by smashing his ankle while knocking the dirt from his spikes.

Look under "D" for "Doctor" and "Dimwit"

Steve Sparks was open to suggestions. As a pitcher in the Brewers organization during the early nineties, he wasn't going far, having never risen above AA until the team suggested that he learn to throw a knuckleball. He did, and it eventually got him to the majors.

His journey might have been quicker, but during training camp in '94, a group of motivational speakers came to the team and suggested to players that they were capable of anything if they put their minds to it. The speakers made their point by bending iron bars and ripping phone books in half. Sparks was pumped up by the presentation and took their suggestion to heart. The next day he and a few of his teammates tried to test their own strength with the Phoenix Yellow Pages. He got halfway through the big yellow book when he dislocated his left shoulder. If he had only gotten a little further, he might have found the number for a good physical therapist.

Gesundheit

Cubs outfielder Sammy Sosa once threw out his back while sneezing. Sosa was in the Chicago clubhouse, when he sneezed twice, reaggravating a prior injury and sending the slugger to the DL. Sadly, Sosa wasn't the only player snagged by sneezing spasms. Juan Gonzalez, Marc Valdes, and Goose Gossage all missed time after being struck down by a sniffle.

Traditional
Stuff

JERRY Seinfeld once lamented that in the age of free agency we're all pretty much "rooting for laundry," as the rival player mercilessly booed today might very well be the home team's starting center fielder next year. If the roster you root for this year bears no resemblance to next year's twenty-five-man squad, and on top of it, your team has adopted a special commemorative alternative retro jersey, who or what are you even a fan of?

What connects our teams from year to year are no longer the names on the back of the jerseys, but a sort of people's history that, over time, has given each stadium its own game-day culture. Each team's fan base has a system of accepted behaviors, a language of shared references, and a collection of obscure players, personalities, and facts.

HOME-FIELD ADVANTAGE

Through its varied experiences and regional flavorings (and occasionally at the behest of its marketing department), every club has a way of doing things—its own quirks, traditions, and truths that serve to distinguish it in the eyes of its faithful followers from all others. The players may change, but the chanting cadence of the crowd stays the same. As does the seventh-inning-stretch sing-along and the random, trivia-worthy features that no championship ever hinged upon, but every real fan knows. Here's a rundown from around the league.

Clap-Clap, Clap-Clap-Clap—New York, AL

Love them (by being one of them) or hate them (by being anyone else), Yankee fans have one of the best fan rituals in professional sports. The role call that precedes each Yankee home game connects the fans with the team in a way that perfectly captures the relationship between the players and their city. "We will chant your name in unison, heap fame and privilege upon you, and make you a star (if not a legend). In return, you will tip your cap and acknowledge us . . . or else."

Originating with the "bleacher creatures" of what was Section 39 of the old stadium, the routine is simple enough. Once the home team takes the field, fans work their way around the diamond chanting each player's name until he responds.

Yankee Stadium has several musical traditions as well. Among them are the playing of "God Bless America" during the seventh-inning stretch, "New York, New York" after games (Sinatra on a good day, Liza Minnelli on occasion for no known reason), and the sounding of Westminster Chimes for each play that results in a Yankee run crossing the plate.

Gosh, you guys are swell cheering on the new guy.
And here I thought Yankee fans were a horrible bunch
of whiny, angry, know it alls.

154

One of the more peculiar numbers to come out of the stadium is the choreographed performance of the disco classic "YMCA" by the grounds crew as they tend to the infield during the fifth inning. Kicked off in 1996 during spring training, the routine migrated north and debuted in the Bronx during a snowy opening day that same year.

Playing Ball North
of the Border—Toronto

They may not sing the standards in Toronto, but Canadian fans are so "OK" with their Blue Jays that they need to belt it out from the rooftops and bleachers during the seventh-inning stretch.

"OK Blue Jays" is the team's official anthem—a fun ode to the game and the home team that's reminiscent of Terry Cashman's "Willie, Mickey, and the Duke (Talkin'

Baseball)." The song, whose performance is credited to the Batboys, was written by Keith Hampshire and first released in 1983. It made its debut at the Sky Dome in 1985, during the ALCS. The chorus makes it the perfect stadium song, with a crowd response built in: "OK *OK*, Blue Jays *Blue Jays*, Let's *Let's*, Play *Play*, Ball!" It also serves to put several American League teams on notice, made all the more fun by a reference to the Brewers, who are now in the National League.

What's most important about the song and the tradition is that it's 100% baseball, which can't be said about the occasional "Aaarrr-goes . . ." chant that surfaces during uneventful game stretches. (It's a reference to Toronto's Canadian Football League team, the Argonauts, who play out of the same facility. "Let's Play Ball," indeed.)

Down by the River Charles—Boston

Commemorating the battles of Lexington and Concord, the third Monday in April is tagged as Patriot's Day on New England calendars (also observed in Wisconsin). The date is home to a parade, the Boston Marathon, and the only morning game on the major-league calendar. On and off throughout their early history, and most every season since 1960, the Red Sox have played their part in the festivities with an 11:05 start time.

Morning, noon, or night, if it's the eighth inning at Fenway, it's time for the faithful to rock out to Neil Diamond. Former Red Sox music director Amy Tobey happened to be a fan of "Sweet Caroline," and as a result, a sing-along anthem was born. Other Boston musical traditions include "Tessie" by Dropkick Murphys, "Dirty Water" by the Standells, and Three Dog Night's "Joy to the World."

*The parade and the marathon approach the mound
to discuss pitch selection.*

The Signs, They Are a Changin'—New York, NL

For years, professional sign man Karl Earhardt could be seen from a box-seat behind the third-base dugout at Shea Stadium, flashing his homemade signs (one of the reported sixty he would have prepared for each game). The signs rallied or critiqued the team depending on their performance. (Considering how the team fared more often than not during those early years, it's fair to say he wasn't as popular with the players as he was with his fellow fans.) Perhaps the sign man's most iconic moment followed the team's first World Championship, where he succinctly summed up the miracle team of '69 with, "There Are No Words."

Earhardt's run extended into the early '80s, and while other super fans have followed him (like the Cowbell Man who can be seen walking around every home game, supplying the team with the necessary amount of cow-bell for proper motivation), the Sign Man's last days as a regular feature at Shea coincided with the installation of a stadium tradition as emblematic of the team as it is of the city they play in. The Home Run Apple made its debut in 1980—a 15-foot-tall fiberglass apple that rises out of a wooden top-hat each time a Met player hits a home run. A new apple now rises at Citi Field (the Mets' new stadium), but the original is still on display.

From the Beatles in 1965 to the curtain-call requests introduced to the baseball landscape by fans of the '86 team (where the providers of significant moments were called out of the dugout by the crowd for a tip of the hat), Shea Stadium also boasted something of a musi-cal tradition. The sounds of Shea have occasionally been overpowered by the jets taking off and landing at LaGuardia Airport—the airport and stadium are so

*The sign guy stood up, providing temporary relief
to the Mets' fans behind him.*

close that pilots use Shea as a runway guidepost, making what's known as an "expressway visual approach" when they land by banking left around the outfield wall and heading for Runway 31. When fans can hear the

161

music, they've been treated to in-game selections including the team's standard "Meet the Mets," which was written by super fan Ruth Roberts. A recent attempt to introduce an eighth-inning sing-along played a sour note for many when the team looked to Boston for inspiration and chose "Sweet Caroline." Fortunately, clearer heads prevailed when Neil Diamond was eventually replaced with the Monkees' "I'm a Believer."

The Baltimore Banner

While the singing of the National Anthem doesn't qualify as a ballpark tradition, fans in Baltimore have put their stamp on it with a little hometown emphasis. Those in the know will shout out an "O" for "Orioles" at the beginning of the penultimate verse, "Oh, say does that Star-Spangled Banner yet wave."

Once the O's take the field, it should be no surprise

Garçon! There's a fly ball in my soup.

that the best Baltimore traditions are food related, especially considering the amenities that Camden Yards introduced to the baseball scene. From former first baseman and fan favorite Boog Powell's BBQ, to the tradi-

163

tional Maryland crabs, Camden Yards launched a trend in which those in attendance can leave their seats, walk around, get good food, and still see the game. Fans in Seattle, San Francisco, Pittsburgh, Philadelphia, New York, and any other city fortunate enough to have a new post-Camden Yards ballpark dropped in their backyard should reserve a word of thanks to the designers of Baltimore's stadium.

Town of Tough Guys—Philadelphia

Over its history, the Phillies have incorporated the City of Brotherly Love's landmark attraction, the Liberty Bell, into various game elements—usually involving the ringing of a replica after a home team home run. Beyond that, the city and its fans have always taken pride in their tough-town exterior. The famous boo birds that traditionally rule over Eagles football games once booed and pelted Santa Claus with snowballs during a halftime show. Even the Kiss-Cam that most ballparks flash on the diamond screen between innings (prompting fans caught on camera to kiss) is tough in Philly. It's replaced with a Muscle-Cam that riles up the locals and gets them to pose for each other.

For further evidence of Philly's tough image, look no further than its mascot. The Phillie Phanatic, a fuzzy, green tormentor of the visiting team's fans and players, made his debut in the late '70s. Named for the fans whose impact on opposing pitchers reached legendary heights during the '77 NLCS when Dodger pitcher Burt Hooton was reportedly spooked into four straight walks (three of them with the bases loaded), the Phanatic was a hit with the phaithful. His resume is rounded out with the instigation of a small security scare and having survived an assault by a Hall of Fame manager. The former

*You take that back, Phanatic! Barney the purple
dinosaur is NOT annoying!*

took place during Philadelphia's 2008 championship
season, when a hot dog wrapped in foil and launched
by the Phanatic was found the morning after a game
and believed by security to be a bomb. A controlled

explosion ensured that everyone would be safe from the errant meat projectile.

As for the latter, it was none other than Tommy Lasorda who launched himself at the giant muppet, body-slamming him to the turf. In fairness, at the time the Phanatic was running over a dummy outfitted in a Lasorda jersey. Abusing Lasorda's likeness was something of a hobby for the Phanatic, made easier by Dodger second baseman Steve Sax, who supplied the mascot with jerseys until Lasorda wizened up and stopped packing extras on trips to Philly. The fiery manager hated seeing anything "Dodger blue" treated with disrespect, and on this particular occasion during the 1988 season, he reached his limit, going after not only his tormentor, but also the four-wheeler the Phanatic used to drive around the field.

A Brave New World—Atlanta

Unless you're a cartoon cowboy or an activist, you have nothing to fear when you cross over into Braves' territory and hear the war drums. Late in a game, regardless of whether or not the home team is playing particularly competitive ball that day, whenever a Braves player reaches base, the Atlanta faithful are prompted to do the tomahawk chop while chanting a native battle cry provided by the PA system. For those unfamiliar with the ritual (which originated in Florida with the FSU Seminoles), simply hold your arm up in front of your body at a ninety-degree angle, and play a round of Air Whack-A-Mole, extending and contracting to the beat. The move is sometimes facilitated by the purchase of a foam tomahawk.

Some fans should just watch the game at home.

169

The Beat of a Different Drummer—Cleveland

The best home-team traditions are the ones credited to diehard fans, so while the tomahawk chop in Atlanta may occasionally be the subject of scorn, you have to tip your hat to John Adams and his drum. For over thirty years, Adams has pounded away at Indians' home games from the last row of the left-center-field stands, surviving the move to a new ballpark and countless disappointing seasons in between. Adams has purchased two tickets—one for himself and one for his drum—for every home game since 1973. (It has been reported that he's been to all but thirty-four games).

The big, bass drum, dubbed "Big Chief Boom-Boom" by Herb Score (the Indians' announcer), has brought national attention to its player—including a bobble-head doll and an award from the Baseball Reliquary, honoring him as one of the game's all-time great fans.

Take Me Out to the
Ball Game—Chicago, NL

It has been over one hundred years since Jack Norworth first wrote of Katie Casey's desire for someone to "Take Me Out to the Ball Game," but it wasn't until Harry Carey (who was broadcasting for the White Sox at the time) was prompted by team owner Bill Veeck to sing it during the seventh-inning stretch that the song became a real ballpark tradition. Veeck argued that if someone with a voice as bad as Carey's could sing it, anyone could (and would). Carey's tradition is of course associated with Wrigleyville, as he took his act with him when he left the South Side and took his place in Cubs' lore. Harry's sing-alongs were as much a part of a trip to Wrigley as the ivy-covered outfield walls and throwing back onto the field the visiting team's home-run balls. Following his passing, the song played on, with visiting celebrities and special guests leading the crowd.

Beer and Sausage Running Wild—Milwaukee

If you fell asleep in a pub and had the dream of all dreams, it might involve delicious meat snacks running in circles—hot dogs, chorizo, bratwurst, along with Italian and Polish sausages all making a mad dash for glory while mustached beer brewers slide into giant mugs of beer. No, this isn't heaven: it's Miller Park in Milwaukee. And the only thing that can spoil the sausage races is Randall Simon (the former Pirate first baseman who once took a bat to the Italian sausage). While the races are a regular event, held each home game during the bottom of the sixth, Bernie the

The wiener of this game will advance to the World Series.

Brewer's sudsy splashdowns are reserved for Brew-crew home runs.

Reds on Parade—Cincinnati

In Cincinnati, like the rest of the country, Opening Day is a holiday. But for the past eighty-plus years, Red fans have stepped it up with a parade worthy of the occasion. The Findlay Market Parade is a sea-of-red celebration of the team and the city, rolling through the downtown streets prior to the season's first pitch. As a member of the senior circuit, the Reds are extended the courtesy of opening each season at home—making the first Monday in April a date worth scheduling some hooky from work or school.

Campaign Contributions—Washington DC

The Nationals haven't been in DC long enough to be

deep-rooted in tradition, but if there's one thing that can rev up a DC crowd, it's a presidential race. With Mount Rushmore represented on the starting line, Washington, Jefferson, Lincoln, and Roosevelt challenge each other during the fourth inning of home games in a run through the capitol city, finishing up at home plate. The races started at old RFK Stadium and made their way over to Nationals Park, where despite a change of scenery, Teddy has yet to finish first.

Before the Nationals were transplanted to Washington, they were the Montreal Expos. Almost thirty years in Olympic Stadium gave rise to the incomparable Youppi, a shaggy, plush mascot who inspired Expo rooters to clang their chairs in support of the home team. While he/she/it was no Bobby Cox, Youppi did bear the distinction of being tossed out of a game by an umpire—an incident prompted by Dodger manager

Tommy Lasorda's complaints (putting the giant fuzz ball in good company with the Phillie Phanatic, another object of Lasorda's mascot-driven scorn).

TRADITIONAL TRADITIONS

Some ballpark traditions come from enthusiastic fans, others from original (if not clever) marketing. But if imitation is a mark of flattery, then the only question is who gets flattered first.

The following features have been passed around and picked up.

Races

In addition to presidents and sausages, the middle-inning racing memo seems to have made its way around the majors. In New York, subways and airplanes have raced on the big screen. In Minnesota, it's three fishermen (actually two fishermen and one fisherwoman) competing to see who can bring in the biggest haul. While in Pittsburgh, racing pierogies go from the big screen to the outfield to determine dumpling supremacy.

Theme Music

While the Yankees have "New York, New York" and the Red Sox are known for their "Dirty Water," some other team tunes include: "New York State of Mind" (Mets); "I Left My Heart in San Francisco" (Giants); "I Love LA" (Dodgers); "Rocky Mountain Way" (Rockies); "Deep in the Heart of Texas" (Astros); *The Dukes of Hazard* theme song (Braves); and "Gonna Fly Now" (Phillies).

Mascots

With several of them mentioned already, it seems that, as a species, mascots have evolved along several distinct family lines. Here is a list of groupings along with the "creatures" associated with each:

HEADS FOR BASEBALL: Mr. Met (New York, NL); Mr. Redlegs (Cincinnati); Homer (Atlanta)

FURRY MONSTERS: Philly Phanatic (Philadelphia); Gapper (Cincinnati); Southpaw (Chicago, AL); Slider (Cleveland); Wally the Green Monster (Boston); Rally (Atlanta)

SEA LIFE: Billy the Marlin (Florida); Lou Seal (San Francisco); Raymond, the Sea Dog/Manatee hybrid (Tampa Bay)

PROFESSIONAL RALLY STARTERS: Captain Jolly Roger (Pittsburgh); Bernie the Brewer (Pittsburgh); the Swinging Friar (San Diego)

MAMMAL MASCOTS: D. Baxter the Bobcat (Arizona); Junction Jack, the Rabbit (Houston); Mariner Moose (Seattle); Paws, the Tiger (Detroit); Rangers Captain, the Horse (Texas); Slugerrr, the Lion (Kansas City); Stomper, the Elephant (Oakland); T.C. Bear (Minnesota)

FEATHERED FRIENDLIES: The Famous Chicken (San Diego); Ace, the Blue Jay (Toronto); The Bird (Baltimore); Fred Bird, the Red Bird/Cardinal (St. Louis); Screech, the Bald Eagle (Washington DC)

EXTINCT: Youppi (formerly of Montreal, current whereabouts unknown); Dandy (a Yankee-doodle mascot, who, rumor has it, was beaten out of the Bronx by angry fans); Dinger (a stegosaurus still active in Colorado)

I lost my lunch, in San Francisco.

Pepper Games Allowed

In the game of pepper, several players will gather around a batter and use their quickest reflexes to keep a ball in play between them. It's generally outlawed by team officials, as it risks injury and unnecessarily wears down the field. With no such restrictions, here are some final quick hits.

ANAHEIM ANGELS OF LOS ANGELES: The Rally Monkey has a specific series of game-related rules that must be honored before he can make an appearance.

TAMPA BAY RAYS: The Tropicana Dome lights up orange at night following home wins.

SAN FRANCISCO GIANTS: A cable car bell rings for each Giant run scored in their half inning.

PIRATES: The wall in right field is 21 feet high, honoring Pittsburgh's beloved right fielder, #21 Roberto Clemente.

References

Books

Bradley, Mickey and Dan Gordon. *Haunted Baseball.* The Lyons Press, 2007.

Nelson, Kevin and Bob Wolff. *So Hank Says to Yogi….* Chamberlain Bros., 2005

Nemec, David and Scott Flatow. *Great Baseball Feats, Facts & Firsts.* New American Library, 2008.

Neyer, Rob. *Rob Neyer's Big Book of Baseball Legends.* Fireside, 2008.

Pahigan, Josh and Kevin O'Connell. *The Ultimate Baseball Road Trip.* The Lyons Press, 2004.

Smith, H. Allen and Ira L. Smith. *Low and Inside.* Breakaway Books, 2000.

Smith, H. Allen and Ira L. Smith. *Three Men on*

Third. Breakaway Books, 2000.

Sullivan, George. *Baseball's Boneheads, Bad Boys & Just Plain Crazy Guys.* Millbrook Press, 2003.

Voigt, David. *American Baseball.* Pennsylvania State University Press, 1979.

Newspapers and Magazines

Bechtel, Mark. "Knuckling Down: Hard-luck Steve Sparks has taken a wobbly path to the Angels' rotation," *Sports Illustrated*, July 13, 1998.

Boswell, Thomas. "The Weird, Wacky World of Baseball Injuries," *The Washington Post*, May 19, 2004.

Durso, Joseph. "Mets Clinch Tie for Title but Lose Ojeda for Season; Pitchers Fingers Severely Cut," *The New York Times*, September 22, 1988.

Jenkins, Lee. "Life in a Cage: Baby Sleeps, Mom Cooks, Dad Bats," *The New York Times*, July 1, 2007.

Nightengale, Bob. "Pair of pitchers from India eye major league opportunities," *USA Today*, November 4, 2008.

Mallozzi, Vincent. "Cheering Section; Recalling the Times of the Signs at Shea," *The New York Times*, June 18, 2006

Weese, Bryn. "Topless woman at Jays game," *Ottawa Sun*, July 15, 2008.

AP Staff. "Royals OF shoots reporter with pellet." Associated Press, July 28, 2007

Websites

www.baseball-reference.com

Dotson, Chad. "Redleg Nation Radio, Episode 2." www.redlegnation.com/2006/07/27/redleg-nation-radio-episode-2/#comments

ESPN Page 2 Staff. "Biggest Cheaters in Baseball."

www.espn.go.com/page2/s/list/cheaters/ballplayers.html

Holloman, Ray. "All-Bizarre Injury Team." http://sports.espn.go.com/espn/print?id=1347109&type=page2Story

Index